Michio Fujioka

Photographs by Shigeo Okamoto

KYOTO

Translated by Bruce A. Coats

COUNTRY RETREATS
The Shugakuin and Katsura Palaces

KODANSHA INTERNATIONAL LTD.

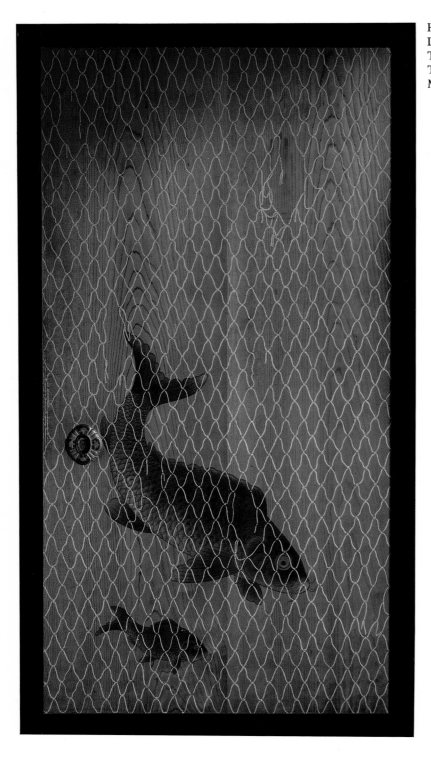

Half-title page: Stream and garden in front of the First Room of the Jugetsukan, Shugakuin Lower Villa.
Title page: Shelves of Mist in the First Room of the Guest House, Shugakuin Middle Villa.
This and facing page: Metal fittings and decorated panels from the Guest House, Shugakuin Middle Villa.

All color and black and white garden and architecture photos by Shigeo Oka-moto except page 34, the Kyoto tea house. Drawing of Katsura on page 33 by Maya Reiner, courtesy of William Turnbull and Charles Moore.

Distributed in the United States by Kodansha International/USA Ltd., through Harper & Row, Publishers, Inc., 10 East 53rd Street, New York, New York 10022.

Published by Kodansha International Ltd., 12-21 Otowa 2-chome, Bunkyo-ku, Tokyo 112 and Kodansha International/USA Ltd., with offices at 10 East 53rd Street, New York, New York 10022 and at The Hearst Building, 5 Third Street, Suite No. 430, San Francisco, California 94103.

ISBN 4-7700-1102-4 (in Japan)

Library of Congress Cataloging in Publication Data
Fujioka, Michio, 1908-
    Kyoto country retreats.
    (Great Japanese art)
    Includes bibliography.
    1. Kyoto (Japan)—Palaces.   2. Gardens, Japanese—
Japan—Kyoto.   3. Shugakuin Rikyū (Kyoto, Japan)
4. Katsura Rikyū (Kyoto, Japan)   I. Okamoto, Shigeo.
II. Title.   III. Series.
NA7757.F79   1983   725'.17'0952191   83-47619
ISBN 0-87011-602-9

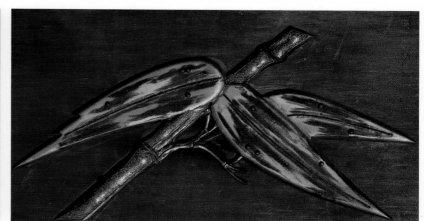

 (continued)

CONTENTS

The Imperial Taste in Palaces   33

Gomizunoo and His Shugakuin   35

The Evolution of Katsura   37

Shugakuin: Splendor in the Hills   38

Katsura: The Perfection of Site
and Structure   42

The Pleasures and Surprises
of the Garden   46

Bibliography   48

2. First Room of the Jugetsukan, Shugakuin Lower Villa.

◁ 1. Garden path leading to the Jugetsukan, Shugakuin Lower Villa.

3. Stream in front garden of the Jugetsukan, Shugakuin Lower Villa.

4. Tree-lined path leading to Shugakuin Upper Villa.

5. Roofed platform on north side of the Rin'untei, Shugakuin Upper Villa.

6. View overlooking the pond from the Rin'untei, Shugakuin Upper Villa.

7. Imperial Dais of the Kyūsuitei with view of the Chitosebashi bridge, Shugakuin Upper Villa.

8. The Manshōtō, Chitosebashi bridge, and Yokuryūchi pond, as seen from the Kyūsuitei, Shugakuin Upper Villa. ▷

◁ 9. The Yokuryūchi pond of Shugakuin Upper Villa
in winter, with the Kyūsuitei at center right.

10. Eastern facade of the restored Shoin buildings and the New Palace, as seen from the Nakajima, Katsura.

11. Palanquin Entry leading to the Old Shoin, Katsura.

12. Moon-viewing platform and pond, as seen from the Second Room of the Old Shoin, Katsura. ▷

13. Interior of the Middle Shoin, Katsura.

14. Staggered shelves (*chigaidana*) and Imperial Dais of the First Room of the New Palace, Katsura.

15. The Musical Instrument Room and Middle Shoin, as seen from the New Palace, Katsura.

16. Veranda of the New Palace leading to the First Room (at right), Katsura. ▷

17. The First Room of the Shōkintei, Katsura.

18. The Ama no Hashidate and Shōkintei, as seen from the northeast shore of the pond, Katsura. ▷

◁ 19. The pond and Ama no Hashidate, as seen from
the First Room of the Shōkintei, Katsura.

21. The northern facade of the Shōiken, Katsura.

22. Dirt-floored loggia of the Shōiken, Katsura.

23. View of the interior of the First Room of the Gepparō, Katsura.

24. Southern facade of the Gepp*arō*, Katsura.

KYOTO COUNTRY RETREATS
The Shugakuin and Katsura Palaces

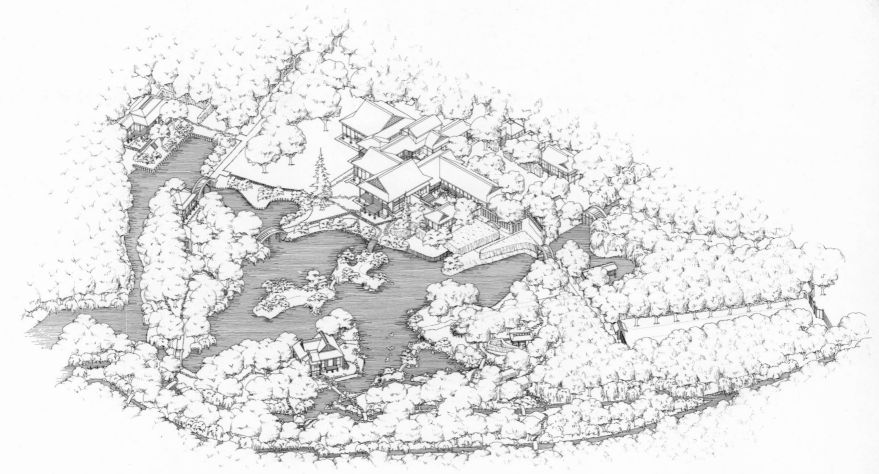

The Katsura Detached Palace.

THE IMPERIAL TASTE IN PALACES

Near Japan's old capital city of Kyoto are two famous country retreats built by members of the Japanese imperial family. Constructed in the seventeenth century, these "detached palaces" of Shugakuin and Katsura share many characteristics and differ in many important aspects. Their most fundamental differences are due to the location and topography of their sites. Shugakuin stands high and dry on the lower slopes of Mount Hiei to the northeast of Kyoto, whereas Katsura lies in a low damp area along the Katsura River southwest of the city.

Shugakuin Rikyū, as the palace is formally known, was situated in the foothills of Mount Hiei to take advantage of the extraordinary beauty of the area with its fine views of the city and the distant mountains to the north and west. In preparing the site, a nearby stream was diverted to flow among the hills, creating a large pond with several islands. The adjacent forested slopes together with the panoramic prospects serve as backdrops for the designed garden, making it seem larger and truly a part of its natural setting. This kind of landscape garden planning in which external elements are actively incorporated into the garden design is called *shakkei*, or "borrowed scenery." Shugakuin is considered one of the finest examples of this technique, and it is noted as well for comprising three separate villas or compounds, each one on a different elevation. By contrast, Katsura Rikyū appears more self-contained, almost ignoring its location along the Katsura River. A large pond was excavated, and the soil removed was used to create artificial hills and islands. Numerous rocks, trees, and shrubs were also brought onto the property. We can therefore say that Katsura is a wholly man-made garden, unlike Shugakuin,

whose form and effect depend greatly on the natural condition of the site.

We can continue in this way, contrasting these two country estates and also identifying their similarities. Shugakuin was largely the work of one man, the retired emperor Gomizunoo (1596–1680; reigned 1611–29). Katsura was assembled by two generations of imperial princes of the Hachijō line, Prince Toshihito (1579–1629) and Prince Toshitada (1619–62), who were uncle and cousin to Gomizunoo. Funding for the construction of Shugakuin came from the controlling military government of the Tokugawa family. Although such information for Katsura is not entirely clear, we know that significant financial support was provided for its construction by Prince Toshitada's in-laws, the wealthy and powerful Maeda family.

People familiar only with European imperial villas might expect that these Japanese detached palaces are extravagantly decorated complexes. Both Shugakuin and Katsura, however, are noted for the simplicity of their designs. From earliest times, the Japanese people have consistently chosen the plain and simple over the highly elaborate. Particularly in the planning of country retreats, or *bessō*, the Japanese have tended to build unornamented informal environments, quite distinct from their urban homes. The Shugakuin and Katsura detached palaces are both typical imperial *bessō* and are often cited as the foremost examples of the Japanese taste for simplicity and refinement. To understand why this is so, we must look at the period of history in which they were built.

The Japanese emperors have been quite different from most European kings and queens in that they have reigned but seldom ruled, having considerable personal prestige but holding no political power.

Detail of six-panel folding screen showing Edo Castle as it appeared ca. the 1640s. (National Museum of Japanese History)

Kyoto teahouse interior from the mid-1700s.

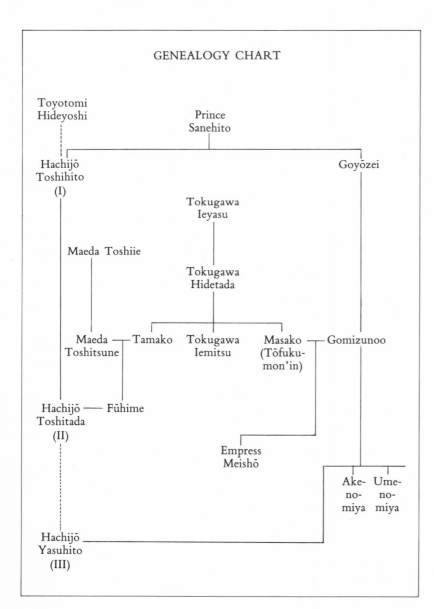

GENEALOGY CHART

This has been true since the late Heian period, around the eleventh century. In the fifteenth and sixteenth centuries, civil war ravaged the country. Kyoto was nearly destroyed, and the emperors stood by powerless as the Kyoto Imperial Palace fell into ruins, for they lacked the resources to maintain the grounds and the buildings. When the country was finally reunified at the end of the 1500s, the new military leaders immediately set about reconstructing the palace, hoping that by supporting the imperial institutions they could enhance the legitimacy of their governments. Three successive rulers, Oda Nobunaga (1534–82), Toyotomi Hideyoshi (1536–98), and Tokugawa Ieyasu (1542–1616), each provided a palace for the reigning emperor of the time.

The emperor and the imperial court devoted a great deal of their time to pursuit of cultured leisure activities. Whereas the warlords, despite their extraordinary powers, were unable to travel freely throughout the country for reasons of personal security, Gomizunoo, Prince Toshihito, and other members of the imperial family, who had not been directly involved in the political struggles of the period, could still venture safely out into the surrounding countryside for occasional amusements. The ruling Tokugawas tried to re-create the natural scenery of the countryside within the protective perimeters of their castle walls; these "rural compounds" (*yamazatomaru*) contained streams, hills, groves, and small pavilions where the military men could relax in safety. Meanwhile, the courtiers ventured out for day or overnight trips and enjoyed boating, moon-viewing, the hillsides, the changes of season. It was for these purposes, in fact, that Shugakuin and Katsura were developed, and later, as peace spread throughout the land, even the wealthier, provincial warlords could start constructing country retreats in their own territories. Aristocrats in general had far fewer resources and could not afford on their own to make their properties very elaborate.

The seventeenth century was also a time of great popularity for

Portrait of the Retired Emperor Gomizunoo. (Reigenkō-ji)

Sculpture of Tōfukumon'in. (Kōun-ji)

The pond in the Sentō Palace garden, Kyoto.

the tea ceremony. Strongly influenced by Zen-sect Buddhism and the asceticism of the monastery, the tea ceremony as it came to be practiced by aristocrats and literati of the time had accumulated philosophical, religious, social, and artistic overtones. Above all, it valued refined behavior, understatement, and an appreciation for plain "artless" objects and settings. Teahouses were built like rustic retreats in carefully tended naturalistic settings. Garden paths leading to these teahouses were designed to be in harmony with their settings and to encourage guests to the ceremony to forget the cares of the everyday world and arrive in the proper state of mind. Conversations would follow prescribed themes focused on the seasons, on literature, and on the utensils used by the teamaster. Tea taste came to represent a broad approach to living, erudition, and the appreciation of nature and everyday objects.

Against this kind of background—war, the dependence of the imperial institutions on the military governors for financial support, and the aesthetic of the tea ceremony—it was natural that imperial country retreats would shun ostentation and develop along more simple and refined lines. We can see elements of this aesthetic in the pathways, structures, and decorative styles of Shugakuin and Katsura. And we shall see as well that the designers of these country retreats could also be bold enough to make exceptions to this general character.

GOMIZUNOO AND HIS SHUGAKUIN

Gomizunoo was the third son of Emperor Goyōzei (reigned 1586–1611) and succeeded his father as emperor. Actually Goyōzei had intended to abdicate in favor of his younger brother, Prince Toshihito. The prince was a man of unusual talent, a typical literati of the Japanese court who in his youth had been adopted by the previous military dictator, Toyotomi Hideyoshi, as his heir. When Hideyoshi fathered his own son in 1589, Toshihito stepped aside

willingly and for doing so was rewarded with designation as the first generation of a new branch of the imperial family, the Hachijō line. He was later given the property at Katsura for his retirement. After Hideyoshi died in 1598, a political power struggle ensued, resulting in the extermination of the Toyotomi family by the Tokugawas. Tokugawa Ieyasu was naturally suspicious of Prince Toshihito, knowing his former connections, and installed Gomizunoo as emperor instead.

The Tokugawa leaders hoped to control the young new emperor, who was just fifteen years old, but Gomizunoo greatly disliked such manipulation. In the past it had been customary for an empress to be selected from among the daughters of ranking courtiers, to which group the warrior Tokugawas did not of course belong. The shogun Tokugawa Hidetada nevertheless arranged in 1620 for his daughter Masako (1607–78), Ieyasu's granddaughter, to be Gomizunoo's consort and empress, thus creating strong ties between the ruling family and the imperial house. Emperor Gomizunoo was distressed by such outside pressures and grew increasingly resentful of continually mounting Tokugawa tyrannies. In 1629, he unexpectedly abdicated, giving the throne to his seven-year-old daughter by Masako. This sudden action surprised both the court and the government, since a woman had not reigned in Japan for over 800 years. The succession, however, obviously pleased the Tokugawas, and the tensions between ruler and Gomizunoo quickly relaxed. The appreciative shogun built a new palace complex for the retired emperor and Masako (now called Tōfukumon'in) adjacent to and southeast of the Kyoto Imperial Palace. This retirement residence was named the Sentō Palace (Sentō Gosho). Here Gomizunoo could escape the public ceremonies and imperial duties which had made his life so unpleasant.

As retired emperor at the age of thirty-three, Gomizunoo now had the opportunity to pass his days in leisure and elegance. Over the next ten to fifteen years, in order to conceal his still-lingering

Trimmed hedge on outer face of pond embankment, Shugakuin Upper Villa.

Odaki waterfall, Shugakuin Upper Villa.

Embankment along western side of Yokuryūchi pond, Shugakuin Upper Villa.

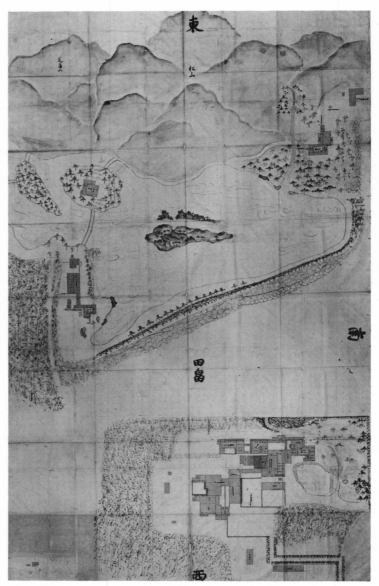

Plan of Upper and Lower villas of Shugakuin, produced sometime before 1682. (Imperial Household Agency)

animosity toward the military dictators, Gomizunoo frequently left Kyoto on short excursions into the countryside. It was during this time that he began planning a country retreat and actively looking for a proper site on which to build it. The land at Shugakuin northeast of the city was particularly pleasing to the retired emperor. Geographically, the area was one of hills and forests and fields. More important, perhaps, was that it was also the site of a Buddhist nunnery, Enshō-ji, where Gomizunoo's first daughter, Ume-no-miya (1619–97), lived. This imperial princess had been born to one of Gomizunoo's consorts prior to Masako becoming empress, and had retired to Enshō-ji to escape the attention of the Tokugawa government. The retired emperor built a small teahouse called Rin'untei (Pavilion among the Clouds) on a hilltop near Enshō-ji, probably so that he could combine visits to the nunnery with his pleasure trips into the countryside. The Tokugawa government was happy to help Gomizunoo develop the area at Shugakuin into a spacious retreat. The teahouse Rin'untei became its nucleus, while the Enshō-ji nunnery was moved to another location where Ume-no-miya could lead her life in quiet seclusion.

The present Shugakuin as administered by the Imperial Household Agency is composed of three areas—the Upper, Middle, and Lower villas. The Middle Villa is a later addition and did not figure into the initial plans. We have very few detailed records on the actual construction of Shugakuin, but work—whether under Gomizunoo's direct supervision or not no one really knows—seems to have been conducted in three phases. During the first phase of work, the Lower Villa with its gardens and buildings was constructed. Completed in the spring of 1659, it was available for use while the second phase of construction was carried out on the Upper Villa. There, just below the Rin'untei, a long embankment was raised across a small valley and a stream diverted to flood the area, forming a large pond. The retaining bank measures over 200 meters in length and about 15 meters

Portrait of Prince Toshihito. (Jishō-in)

Portrait of Prince Toshitada. (Imperial Household Agency)

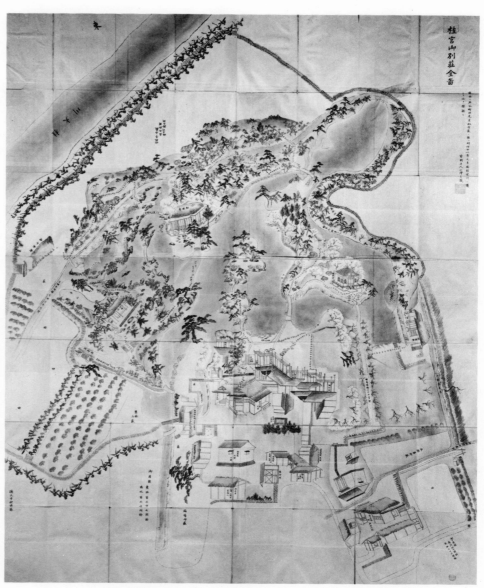
Plan of Katsura, drawn ca. 1700 and reproduced 1888. (National Diet Library)

in height on the downhill side, which is built up of four-tiered stone walls. This extraordinary project was completed in 1661.

The third phase of work at Shugakuin involved the construction of the waterfall that is called Odaki (Male Waterfall). The upper reaches of the Otowa River which lay to the west were diverted and brought by conduit to a spot in the ravine east of the Rin'untei. Work on the waterway and falls continued for about two years. Based on old drawings of the area, we know that the present configuration of the Odaki is much smaller than what Gomizunoo planned. It is nevertheless still a lovely spot to visit. Shugakuin is today justly admired for the way it exploits the natural contours of its mountain site in its landscape. But achieving that harmony was no easy feat. Most people merely strolling along Shugakuin's many delightful paths probably do not realize just how truly large-scale a construction project the embankment, pond, and other features actually represent. Certainly, without the financial assistance of the Tokugawa government Shugakuin could never have been built.

Gomizunoo greatly loved Shugakuin and went there often. The views of rice fields layered up the hillside between the Lower and Upper villas were pronounced to be particularly delightful. It is said that when Gomizunoo first started coming to Shugakuin, the Tokugawa government insisted on sending along numerous warriors to serve as his personal bodyguards. Obviously, this protection restricted the retired emperor's movements and destroyed the tranquillity of the site. Gomizunoo sent a personal letter directly to the shogun, saying that he didn't need bodyguards because the people of the country felt no animosity toward him. Thereafter, the service was stopped. The fact that Gomizunoo dealt directly with the government leaders and felt no need for protection from his subjects says a good deal about the position of the retired emperor and imperial court in Japan at that time.

Additional pavilions at Shugakuin now make up the Middle Villa

of the estate and were the residential quarters of Princess Ake-no-miya, another of Gomizunoo's daughters. After Gomizunoo died in 1680, Ake-no-miya became a nun and built a small temple on this site so dear to her father. Called the Rinkyū-ji (Temple Near the Forest), it includes a worship hall constructed in 1682 and other buildings, one of which, the Guest House (Kyakuden), was donated and moved here from the former private apartments of Tōfukumon'in at the Sentō Palace. In 1884 the Rinkyū-ji gave part of its temple grounds to the Imperial Household Ministry (now Agency) to include in the Shugakuin Detached Palace complex. The buildings of this Middle Villa, not being part of the original scheme, provide an interesting contrast to the Upper and Lower sites, and they add effectively to this country retreat's particular characteristic of small buildings and gardens scattered among the fields and forest at the foot of Mount Hiei. Although we might consider Shugakuin today as being comparatively close to its original seventeenth-century form, we must remember that major changes have taken place since its construction. Several buildings have been lost, additions made, and restorations needed. We will discuss these details later in the text.

THE EVOLUTION OF KATSURA

As we recall, Prince Toshihito was the younger brother of Emperor Goyōzei and particularly well suited in temperament to become emperor, although in the end it was Gomizunoo who was installed. As the first generation of the new Hachijō branch of the imperial family, Toshihito was given lands along the Katsura River, and it was here that he decided to build a country retreat. Unfortunately, at that time the Katsura estate produced only 3,000 koku of rice (1 koku = 180 liters). This being hardly sufficient to finance the construction of a large bessō, Katsura in its earliest stages was quite modest. The river itself provided much of the recreation. This area

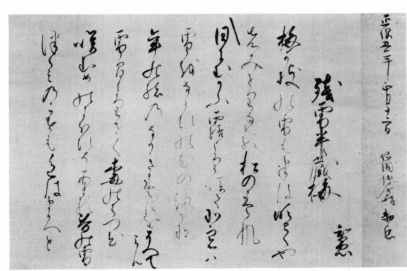

Four poems presented by Toshitada at Gomizunoo's New Year's poetry party, 1649, on the theme "Half-open Plum Blossoms on Lingering Snow." The poem favored by the retired emperor is marked with a slash:

> Blossoming from the dew,
> They reach for the sun.
> The north-facing window,
> A string to frame
> Snowlike blossoms.

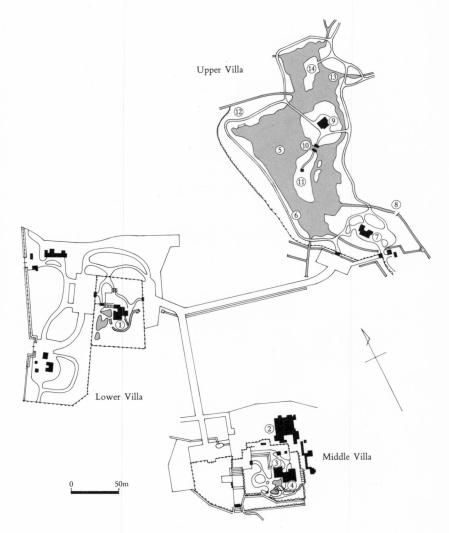

Map of Shugakuin Detached Palace.
(1) Jugetsukan. (2) Rinkyū-ji. (3) Rakushiken. (4) Guest House. (5) Yokuryūchi. (6) Embankment. (7) Rin'untei. (8) Odaki waterfall. (9) Kyūsuitei. (10) Chitosebashi bridge. (11) Manshōtō. (12) Site of Shishisai. (13) Maple Valley. (14) Mihojima.

had been a country retreat in the tenth century of the famous Fujiwara family of courtiers, and perhaps traces of this estate still remained in the seventeenth century. It seems likely that Prince Toshihito built the Old Shoin (Koshoin), the oldest part of the present main house, and various teahouses on this same site.

In 1629 Prince Toshihito died, and because his son was then only eleven years old, Katsura fell into disuse. Over the next ten years, the gardens and structures were allowed to deteriorate. In 1642, the second-generation Hachijō, Prince Toshitada, married Fūhime (1621–62), the daughter of Maeda Toshitsune, who was the military governor or *daimyō* of Kaga (now Ishikawa Prefecture) and the most important regional ruler under the Tokugawa regime. From that time, Toshitada began building again at Katsura, presumably with financing from the Maedas. The prince had inherited his father's wit and intelligence, and was well educated in the arts, including tea, and the classical literature of China and Japan. In planning the new Katsura gardens, he was inspired by descriptions of the palatial estates in the eleventh-century tale of court life in Japan, *The Tale of Genji*, and tried to re-create some of its landscape scenery. He enlarged the pond, giving it the serene appearance reminiscent of Heian gardens described in that book. He also arranged rocks and trees with deliberate literary symbolism. Visitors to the estate were delighted by the allusions.

Prince Toshitada added residential quarters, initially extending the Old Shoin with the rooms now referred to as the Middle Shoin (Chūshoin). Much later, in anticipation of a visit by retired emperor Gomizunoo in 1663, the New Palace (Shingoten) was constructed to the west and connected to the main house by the Musical Instrument Room (Gakki no Ma). Prince Toshitada died without an heir in the year before the expected imperial visit, and a son of Gomizunoo, Prince Yasuhito (1643–65), was given the title of third generation of the Hachijō line. The New Palace probably was completed accord-

ing to the plans drawn up by Prince Toshitada. I believe we can also view the teahouse Shōkintei (Pavilion of the Pine Lute) as dating from this time, and another teahouse, the Shōiken (Pavilion of Laughing Thoughts), as being added later.

In this way did Katsura evolve. It was begun as a modest retreat, and gradually expanded and elaborated. The later additions, such as the New Palace and the pond garden near the Shōkintei with its numerous rock arrangements, involved substantial expenditures, and we cannot imagine them without considering the generous financial backing of the Maeda family. The fourth through sixth generations of the Hachijō line were, like Yasuhito, all princes of the imperial family, and died young without heirs. Not until Prince Yakahito (1703–67) was Katsura extensively used. This seventh-generation Hachijō made many repairs to the estate, remodeling walkways and adding a number of stone lanterns. The more or less unified impression Katsura gives us today probably represents the results of Prince Yakahito's renovations.

SHUGAKUIN: SPLENDOR IN THE HILLS

When the retired emperor Gomizunoo was frequenting Shugakuin, this country retreat consisted of only the upper and lower gardens and their pavilions. The two areas were separated by cultivated fields, but were within a few minutes walk of each other. The Lower Villa once contained several structures, of which only the building with the imperial suite remains, albeit an 1824 reconstruction. This is the Jugetsukan (Viewing the Moon of Longevity), and in one corner three floor mats have been raised to serve as the imperial dais. Behind the dais on the west wall is a large alcove (*tokonoma*) for the display of artworks and floral arrangements. Along the north wall is a smaller alcove, where supposedly Gomizunoo stored his lute, and a set of staggered shelves and cabinets (*chigaidana*). Although the birds and

Imperial Gate leading to Shugakuin Lower Villa.

Stone steps ascending to the Rin'untei, Shugakuin Upper Villa.

flowers painted on the cabinet doors add a bright decorative touch, the overall impression of the room is of ornamental restraint and refined simplicity (see plate 2). This type of architecture, in which the natural textures and colors of plaster and wood are highlighted and the construction forms kept quite plain, emulating country farmhouses in accordance with the aesthetic values of the tea ceremony, is called *sukiya* style, and was widely used in the seventeenth century. The east and south walls of the Jugetsukan open onto a small garden canopied with trees and crossed by a meandering stream (see half-title page).

When we enter the Lower Villa from the gate at the northwest corner, we pass some retaining walls, all that remains of the other buildings that at one time were a part of the compound. To our left we see the steps of the Palanquin Entry (Okoshiyose) which lead up to the imperial chambers. Ahead lies a pond with a miniature moss-covered island and several stone slab bridges. On the far side, the path crosses the stream and climbs up to the Jugetsukan (see plate 1). From this walkway, the pavilion has a light, open appearance. The wing closest to the pond is now called Zōrokuan (Hermitage of the Tortoise), although the name was originally given to another building in the compound that has since disappeared. Rooms for retainers and servants have also vanished, but the most important rooms remain as Gomizunoo saw them.

South from the Jugetsukan a path of stepping stones leads to the stream (see plate 3). On the opposite bank is a level area where there once stood a two-story pavilion called Wankyokukaku (Tower at the Bend). On the south side of this site, a few stones remain from a rock and gravel garden. At various spots along the walkways stone lanterns were placed to light the garden at night. Numerous maples grow in the area, and during autumn the crimson and gold-colored leaves are particularly beautiful. All of this created an atmosphere of tranquillity for visitors to enjoy.

Leaving the lower garden, we head directly east and climb a gentle slope to reach the Upper Villa. The roadway is raised above the terraced ricefields and lined on both sides with low pines (see plate 4). The views over the surrounding countryside constantly change as we walk approximately 300 meters to the gate of the upper garden. From this position we can see across the broad valley to the mountains west of Kyoto topped by the peak of Mount Atago. The heart of the Upper Villa is the large pond with its several islands, actually the tops of hills left when the area was flooded. This is called Yokuryūchi (Pond of the Bathing Dragon) from the appearance of these crested isles rising from the water (see plate 9). The long embankment along the west side of the pond makes a gentle curve, and its outer face is densely planted and clipped smoothly across to hide the dike. The pruned azaleas here are exceptionally lovely in bloom. The construction of this enormous pond, equivalent in our time to building a dam to create a lake, was an incredible feat of engineering for its era.

Around the Yokuryūchi are several paths that once connected the various pavilions perched here and there among the hills and islands. At present we find only two buildings remaining, the Rin'untei

View of the pond and surrounding hills from the Rin'untei, Shugakuin Upper Villa.

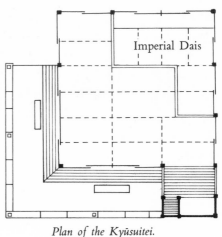

Plan of the Kyūsuitei.

Imperial Dais

The Rin'untei, Shugakuin Upper Villa.

(Pavilion among the Clouds) and Kyūsuitei (Far-Away Pavilion). The Rin'untei stands on a knoll to the south of the pond. It is built in an L-shape with one wing overlooking the entire garden and the other open to the city and eastern hills (see plates 5,6). The westward view across the pond to the mountains beyond is magnificent, with distant Mount Atago looming up as part of the garden designer's composition. This "borrowed scenery" is a particular feature of Shugakuin. Elsewhere the forested foothills of Mount Hiei extend the landscaped garden views in a rich and varied way. Between the Rin'untei and the pond, paths climbing the hillside are enclosed in a large azalea hedge that is trimmed back to reveal the "borrowed" scenery at certain carefully chosen points.

Within the pond are three large islands, the highest center one being crowned with the Kyūsuitei. This pavilion is very simple. The single room measures about 6 meters square, with a small pantry tucked under the eaves at one corner. On two sides, the roof extends over an earth-floored loggia. Inside, a raised matted area along two walls forms an L-shaped dais where the retired emperor could sit and look down over the pond (see plate 7). The window is sheltered outside by a light wooden awning. From here we can see the Chitosebashi (Bridge of a Thousand Years) that leads to the Manshōtō (Isle of Ten Thousand Pines). This bridge, added to the garden in the first half of the nineteenth century, is Chinese in style and consequently somewhat inappropriate to its setting (see plate 8). Looking around the interior of the Kyūsuitei, we do not find the *tokonoma* alcove. This type of room ornament was more typical of the residences built for the warrior class than of those for the court aristocracy, although the use of the *tokonoma* at the Jugetsukan of the Lower Villa indicates just how architectural trends were diffusing by this time. The bare space of the Kyūsuitei, by contrast, exhibits a refined beauty in the simplicity of its form.

Another pavilion, a teahouse, was formerly located on a level site near the northern end of the pond embankment. This was the Shishisai (Retirement Room); in later years it was moved away and now only the foundation stones remain. In front of this structure there was a boat landing where guests using the teahouse could alight from craft carrying them across the pond. Or, they could approach the Shishisai on foot, walking down from the Rin'untei through a shadowy glade, past the waterfall Odaki, to a path that wound around the pond. Strolling north and east, they would bypass the Maple Bridge (Kaedebashi) leading to the middle island with the Kyūsuitei. Instead, they could cross a bridge at Maple Valley (Momijidani), where several streams feeding the pond come splashing down. Continuing around the water's edge to the north shore, they would have a clear

The Kyūsuitei, Shugakuin Upper Villa.

Plaque reading "Rakushiken" modeled on Gomizunoo's written characters.

view of Mihojima (the Island of Miho), an allusion to a famous pine-clad site site in eastern Japan. The scenery in this back area is truly superb in autumn. The trail then rises slightly, opening a view across the broadest part of the pond to the knoll with the Rin'untei and the wooded slopes beyond. The boat landing for the Shishisai lies below.

The Middle Villa of Shugakuin is located to the south of both the Upper and Lower villas and is approached by a long straight roadway lined with pines. We recall that this part of the estate was built by Gomizunoo's daughter Ake-no-miya. The nunnery of Rinkyū-ji still forms the eastern half of this compound and is closed to the public. The several buildings which the Rinkyūji transferred to the Shugakuin Detached Palace in the late nineteenth century include the personal quarters of Ake-no-miya, the Guest House, a kitchen, and a dirt-floored work space. Beneath the eaves of the first pavilion hangs a plaque thought to have been modeled on brushwork done by Gomizunoo when he was seventy-two years old. It reads "Rakushiken" (Pavilion of Ease and Amusement) and was originally made for another building that no longer stands. The building now bearing the name Rakushiken has two rooms facing south onto a pond garden. The First Room (Ichi no Ma) contains a plain *tokonoma* alcove, and the Second Room (Ni no Ma) has a very simple bookshelf and cabinet. The whole suite probably appears as it did in the late seventeenth century.

By dramatic contrast, the Guest House is elaborately decorated. This building had originally been part of the Sentō Palace and was moved here after the deaths of Tōfukumon'in in 1678 and Gomizunoo in 1680. At that time, the arrangement of rooms was slightly altered, with the First Room enlarged and the Second Room set back from the facade about 1 meter. Filling the north wall of the First Room are an adjoining 2-meter-long *tokonoma* at left, and, at right, an extremely complicated set of shelves and cabinets, or *chigaidana* (see

title page). Because the shelves are elegantly staggered and layered, they have been aptly named the Shelves of Mist (Kasumidana). The walls of the *tokonoma* are decorated at top with sheets of poems and paintings pasted over cloud forms of gold dust, and at bottom with a checkerboard pattern of gold and dark blue squares. This colorful design is similar to one we shall see at Katsura. On the veranda connecting the two rooms are several cedar panel doors painted with depictions of the parade wagons of Kyoto's annual Gion Festival. The hardware throughout this building is beautifully crafted (see contents page).

If we wonder where this handsome suite of rooms might have been located at the Sentō Palace of Tōfukumon'in and Gomizunoo, we can consult old floor plans that show long corridors leading from the separate apartment complexes of the retired emperor and empress and meeting up at a single pavilion toward the rear of the compound. Guests would never have reached these private chambers, so we can assume that this area was for the exclusive use of the imperial couple. As Gomizunoo and his empress were well on in years when this pavilion was built, doubtless it was designed in the hope that the colorful and vigorous ornamentation would impart a youthful atmosphere to their meetings. This same mood prevails today at the Guest House of Shugakuin's Middle Villa.

Matched tea bowls with gold and silver patterns made by Nonomura Ninsei and presented to Tōfukumon'in. (MOA Museum)

Map of Katsura Detached Palace.
(1) Front Gate. (2) Imperial Gate. (3) Imperial Visit Walkway. (4) Outer Arbor. (5)
Ama no Hashidate. (6) Shōkintei. (7) Manjitei. (8) Shōkatei. (9) Onrindō. (10) Shōiken.
(11) Plum Paddock. (12) Kemari ground. (13) New Palace. (14) Musical Instrument
Room. (15) Middle Shoin. (16) Old Shoin. (17) Palanquin Entry. (18) Gepparō. (19)
Nakajima. (20) Katsura River.

Gate leading to the Palanquin
Entry, Katsura.

KATSURA: THE PERFECTION OF SITE AND STRUCTURE

The Katsura Detached Palace occupies a low, damp, irregularly shaped
site along the west bank of the Katsura River, about 7 hectares in
size. Roughly at the center of the estate is a long complex waterway filled with numerous large and small islands. To the west of
the pond on higher level ground stand the three main buildings: the
Old Shoin, the Middle Shoin, and the New Palace. Each is set back
from the next in a zigzag plan (see plate 10). Guests entering the
residential quarters were received in the northeast corner of the Old
Shoin at the Palanquin Entry (Okoshiyose). Immediately to the east
is a small pavilion at the water's edge called the Gepparō (Pavilion
of the Moon and Waves) and this is matched on the opposite shore
by the teahouse Shōkintei (Pavilion of the Pine Lute). These two
structures and the eastern end of the pond are probably the most
complexly conceived parts of the Katsura garden. The path connecting them passes by the open-air shelters of the Outer Arbor
(Sotokoshikake) and the Manjitei (Pavilion of the "Buddhist
Swastika"), both designed for purposes of the tea ceremony. On
the crest of the largest island in the pond is a teahouse called the
Shōkatei (Flower Appreciation Pavilion) which replicates the rustic
teashops found along mountain trails. Further west on this island
was built the Buddhist worship hall Onrindō (Hall of the Forest
Park) and across an inlet is the Shōiken (Pavilion of Laughing
Thoughts). When winter comes, through the bare tree branches we
can see all these many structures from the veranda of the main house.

The Old Shoin is the oldest building at Katsura and was constructed
by Prince Toshihito sometime in the late 1610s. Located on land
a bit higher than the rest of the low and damp site, it is the only
wing of the main house with a floor close to the ground. Owing
to the smooth curves of the pond in front and the scattering of visi-
ble small islands, the feeling here is graceful and expansive (see plate
12). Adjoining the Old Shoin and set further back from the pond
is the Middle Shoin, built by the second-generation Hachijō, Prince
Toshitada, as his country home. It is slightly more refined than the
Old Shoin and, in what has become the trademark of Katsura's
architecture, stands high above its foundation stones to escape damp-
ness and possible flooding from the nearby river (see plate 13). Present-
ing a similar aspect further west and stepped back in two segments
are the Musical Instrument Room and the New Palace. While the
New Palace, like the other buildings, looks simple and rustic from
the outside, it is elegantly appointed inside with rare imported woods
and elaborately wrought metal fittings. Such luxury was extravagant
for Katsura but was understandable considering that the wing was
probably added in anticipation of a visit by the retired emperor
Gomizunoo in 1663 (see plates 14–16).

A large lawn extends out from the New Palace almost to the pond.
Tradition says that this broad level plot was cleared for *kemari* games,
a type of kickball popular among courtiers since the Heian period.
The open veranda alongside the Musical Instrument Room supposedly
was built as a gallery for watching the matches. This explanation
must have been formulated in later times, for the wing with the
Musical Instrument Room was more likely a necessary structural
device for elegantly connecting the roofs of the main house with
the New Palace. The veranda serves as an open corridor between
the buildings, and the lawn recalls the flat gravel courtyards that
have traditionally fronted the main halls (*shinden*) of imperial palaces
since the Heian period. Perhaps this was planned as a deliberate allusion for the delight of the visiting retired emperor, playing off the
simple, lighthearted structures of the country house with the more
solemn formality of the New Palace.

The garden pond at Katsura is presently a single body, but in the
past the larger waterway fronting the Old Shoin and the inlet near
the Shōkintei were separated by a stretch of land. They were distinct
ponds. The main pond dates back, perhaps, to around the tenth cen-

Katsura's Shoin buildings, before their recent restoration.

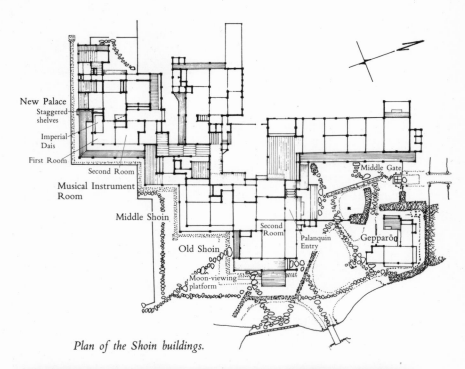

Plan of the Shoin buildings.

tury when the Fujiwara family had a rural retreat here, and, as we noted before, its appearance is reminiscent of the Heian-period gardens described in the *Tale of Genji*. The eastern pond was dug under Prince Toshitada's direction; it is a superb contrast to the older expanse. The shores are lined with a multitude of stones, showing in their arrangements strong influence of the Zen rock gardens which were first developed in Japan during the medieval period (thirteenth–sixteenth centuries). Many stone groupings seem symbolic in configuration. Perhaps the most striking is the expanse of flat black pebbles laid out to suggest a strip of land projecting into the sea. The tip is terminated by a lantern perched on a promontory. Nearby two rock-bound islands are connected by an arcing stone slab and planted with dwarfed pines. The whole composition is said to represent the famous sand spit at Ama no Hashidate ("Bridge of Heaven") in the Tango region along the Sea of Japan. The garden arrangement differs from the actual scenery, though, and is not a miniature version of that coastline. Such a placing of stones to evoke Ama no Hashidate had been a standard landscape garden device in Japan since medieval times. But perhaps this stylized grouping had a special significance at Katsura, for Prince Toshitada's mother was born in Tango.

The best view of this pond is from the Shōkintei, which sits close to the water's edge. On its east side a single slab of granite nearly 6 meters long bridges the pond and connects the teahouse with the garden path. As we walk along this path, making our way to the Shōkintei from the main house, we follow a varied and delightful route. Leaving the area of the Palanquin Entry (see plate 11), we move straight along the pebble pavement of the Imperial Visit Walkway (Miyukimichi) to a break in the hedge at right. Another straight passage leads through the Maple Paddock (Momiji no Baba). Halfway down this walk, we turn left where large stepping stones slow our pace and guide our movements. Soon we reach an open shelter known as the Outer Arbor, its thatched roof protecting a

The Outer Arbor, Katsura.

Path of round and cut
stones leading from the
Outer Arbor, Katsura.

Open hearth (kudozukuri) at the Shōkintei, Katsura.

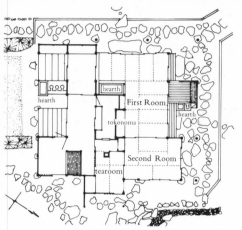

Plan of the Shōkintei.

waiting bench and privy. Here guests to the Shōkintei would assemble and await the call of their host. The path from here continues straight for several meters, paved with an extraordinary combination of rough and cut stones. At the end of this, our way is blocked by a stone lantern, and tall trees behind obscure our view of what lies in the distance. We turn left, stepping down and across a simple stone bridge. Our attention is first attracted by the rhythmic beating of a small waterfall at left. Only now, turning right to resume the path, do we see Ama no Hashidate and the Shōkintei for the first time (see plate 18).

Around the eastern inlet, the stepping stones take us to the water's edge. Here and there large flat rocks allow us to pause and enjoy the sequence of views. The creator of this garden carefully composed these scenes and set the stepping and stopping stones quite deliberately to control our movements and focus our attention. Continuing south we clearly see the Shōkintei and the remarkable stone slab that bridges to it. Among the hills at left stands another waiting shelter, the Manjitei. This walkway is extremely long when compared with the usual garden paths leading to a teahouse, and I doubt that the entire length was designed as a single approach. It rather has the feel of being a collection of various styles of tea-garden paths, and this composite nature makes it seem almost excessive in its artifice.

As the most important structure within Katsura's garden, the Shōkintei teahouse arouses our interest from many different standpoints. Scholars previously believed that the Shōkintei was among the oldest structures at Katsura, but recent investigation indicates that it dates from around the time of the New Palace. The building form is quite complex. On the north side facing the pond, the ground-cover of pebbles and flat stones extends far beneath the eaves. A low open hearth adjoins the plank porch. Built like a kitchen (kudozukuri), such facilities would usually be found at the rear of the building rather

than along the facade. Although the Gepparō also has such an open hearth, this is not a typical feature in country house construction. We may wonder why such a peculiarity is found at Katsura. Perhaps the explanation lies again in the practices of the tea ceremony, in which the host prepares the indoor hearth, boils the water, and whisks a bitter green tea in the presence of his guests. Extending this idea somewhat, the host at the Shōkintei might also have wanted to fix a light meal for his guests to receive and welcome them with the utmost courtesy and good taste. If we ask who it was that the prince intended to entertain here in such a fashion, the answer would have to be retired emperor Gomizunoo. This would date the Shōkintei to the same time as the New Palace, also constructed for the imperial visit of 1663—which, sadly, Toshitada did not live to see. We don't find similar kudozukuri at Shugakuin or any other country retreats built by either courtiers or wealthy warriors of that time. Perhaps the idea of a kitchen hearth on the facade results both from Prince Toshitada's interest in elements of the popular culture and from the aesthetics of the tea ceremony that found special beauty in the commonplace.

The Shōkintei shows characteristics of the refined sukiya style, but it differs from the other buildings at Katsura in its use of some rather bold design features. For example, the main room, the First Room, contains eleven tatami straw floormats arranged in an L-shape around a hearth, cupboards, and tokonoma unit. The walls of this alcove and the partitions adjoining it on the east are covered with a most striking checkerboard pattern of large blue and white paper sheets (see plate 17). The design startles the eye. We recall that a similar pattern on a smaller scale decorated the tokonoma at the Guest House in the Middle Villa at Shugakuin. These bold effects were generally not used in sukiya-style architecture, which stressed restraint in ornamentation. But Gomizunoo liked such inventive features, and the

Trail of stepping stones leading to the Shōkatei, Katsura.

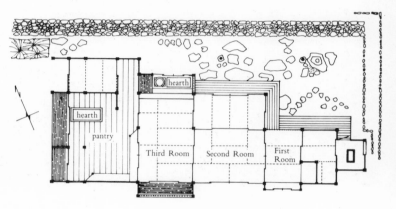

Plan of the Shōiken.

Interior of the Third Room of the Shōiken showing hearth and shelving, Katsura.

Shōkintei decoration would have been most suitable for a guest who was no stranger to the splendors of the imperial palace. The next room to the north of the First Room is more typical of the *sukiya* style. It appears subdued, almost gloomy. The plain interior is hardly equal to the stunning garden of the Ama no Hashidate that it faces, and similarly offers great contrast to the colorful decoration of the adjacent chamber (see plate 19).

At one time in front of the Shōkintei a large red-lacquered bridge crossed over to the opposite shore. Like the Chitosebashi at the Upper Villa of Shugakuin, this decorative bridge would have appeared quite incongruous among the rustic-looking pavilions and other features of the Katsura garden. If we agree that the large pond in front of the Old Shoin and the smaller waterway near the Shōkintei were distinct bodies separated by a strip of land during Prince Toshitada's time, then perhaps we can credit this bridge to the seventh-generation Hachijō, Prince Yakahito, who used the garden extensively throughout his lifetime and made numerous changes to the gardens. We know that many of the stone lanterns located around the pond were added and carefully positioned by the prince to illuminate the garden pathways in the evening. Probably he had the red-lacquered bridge built when the two ponds were joined into one.

To the west of the Shōkintei, cut stones line the shore where boats from the Old Shoin landing could moor. From this point, another path leads around the south side of the garden. Leaving the Shōkintei landing, we follow stepping stones along the shore, cross an earth-covered bridge, and climb a steep hill through a dense grove. We feel that we have entered deep into a mountain forest, and only the occasional glimpse of the main house through the branches belies where we travel. At the peak of this island stands the Shōkatei (Flower Appreciation Pavilion), looking every bit like a tiny teastall of the type often found along mountain trails. In accord with the style of

such open-air reststops, we find *tatami*-padded benches wrapped around three sides of an earth-floored area. At the center is a hearth; again we see the *kudozukuri*, but although the building is plebeian in spirit, the design and craftsmanship are highly refined (see plate 20).

From in front of the Shōkatei, a set of steps descends quickly to a bridge that crosses to the main house. On our left is a Buddhist-style building called the Onrindō where memorial plaques to the members of the Hachijō line are enshrined. Dating from the late seventeenth century, the design differs from that of the other buildings and provides an interesting contrast. Another bridge heads west to a level lawn called the Plum Paddock (Ume no Baba) for the many trees that line the way. At our left is a rectangular cove and on a rise beyond is the Shōiken with its deep eaves and round windows cut out above the entryway (see plates 21, 22). The dirt-floored loggia gives this building, too, the external appearance of a rustic teahouse, but inside the rooms are large and beautifully decorated. The largest room contains an enclosed pantry and hearth at one end with a commodious kitchen adjoining it from which numerous guests could be served. This is quite different from the open hearths at the Shōkintei and Gepparō, and we know that from about the eighteenth century onwards when visitors thronged to see the famous Katsura Detached Palace gardens, a light meal was offered. Possibly the Shōiken was used for that purpose. Until recently, it has been assumed that Prince Toshitada built this pavilion, but since the style seems newer than that of the New Palace and Shōkintei, perhaps the building was added by a later generation.

Returning to the main house, we encounter several straight and randomly set stone paths which mingle and cross. The two varieties of walkways are probably not of the same time period; the straight ones are perhaps more recent additions. Following one of these paths we arrive at the teahouse called Gepparō, northeast of and adjacent

Interior of the Gepparō, Katsura.

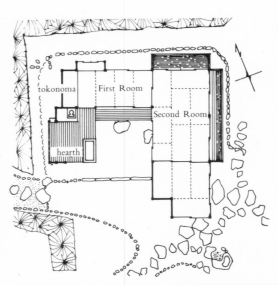

Plan of the Gepparō.

tokonoma First Room

Second Room

hearth

Rockwork in front of the Palanquin
Entry of the Old Shoin, Katsura.

to the Old Shoin (see plates 23,24). Entering under the eaves, we are again in an earth-floored area with an open hearth. In the First Room, a *tokonoma* fills one full wall with a built-in writing desk (*tsukeshoin*) at a right angle and below the window. This is the only room in the Gepparō with a suspended ceiling. Elsewhere we can look up to the exposed bamboo rafters and underside of the roof, as if in a country cottage. From the veranda of the Second Room, we can gaze down on the gently curving shore of the pond. Opposite is the Shōkintei. The scenery is superb, and the building is perfectly sited for moon-viewing. At those times when the moon appears reflected in the water, we know exactly how appropriate is the name Gepparō—''Pavilion of the Moon and Waves.''

Having completed our circuit of the garden, we descend by a few stepping stones to the plot in front of the Palanquin Entry. The rockwork of the walkway here is justly famous. The cut stones are said to be laid in the formal *shin* style favored by the tea master and garden designer Kobori Enshū (1579–1647). In Japanese calligraphy there are three distinct brushwork styles: angular and crisp *shin*, more rounded and softer *gyō*, and abbreviated and loose *sō*. The terms for these styles were also used to describe similar effects in the other arts, and the rockwork in this walk is an outstanding example of the *shin* style being applied to landscape garden design. Recently, scholars have theorized that these stones were not laid by Kobori Enshū himself but were added to the garden many years later as a deliberate reference to his particular style of design.

THE PLEASURES AND SURPRISES OF THE GARDEN

In comparing Katsura and Shugakuin, we have devoted considerable space to their differences, especially as they derive from their sites and the relationship of the gardens to the surrounding areas. Yet we can easily point out their many similarities. Both are a short trip from the heart of Kyoto. Guests could easily travel out for a day's amusements and return by nightfall. Both estates contain large ponds for boating and various pavilions for entertainment. The buildings, for the most part, are simple in design and plain in materials, although beautifully crafted in the refined style of *sukiya* architecture. The ornamental exceptions, at the Guest House of Shugakuin's Middle Villa and at Katsura's New Palace and Shōkintei pavilion, are all structures associated with Gomizunoo and reflect certain flamboyant tastes of the retired emperor.

In 1615 the military government had issued regulations concerning the conduct of the courtier class: the responsibility of the nobility was to exert themselves solely in the pursuit of scholarship and art. By tradition, the imperial family had always pursued cultural activities, but such laws designed to keep the aristocracy out of politics were extraordinary infringements on their freedom. Nevertheless, the role Gomizunoo was expected to play in society must have greatly affected the design at Shugakuin. The retired emperor was an ardent and able practitioner of verse composition and calligraphy, and around his person there always were gathered many of Japan's leading literati. Looking at Shugakuin today we can almost perceive the figure of Gomizunoo leading his cultured life. The pond at the Upper Villa, so artfully enfolding the surrounding mountain landscape, and the excursion boats which floated on its waters were especially meant to call to mind the elegant court life of the bygone Heian age. The atmosphere there remains broad and outreaching. Shugakuin today, to Japanese and foreign observers alike, is easily comprehended and easily appreciated.

Katsura's case is rather more difficult, for it exhibits a stronger influence of the refined tea taste and, as we have said, was assembled over a longer period of time with accompanying complexities. Toshitada's work on the eastern part of the Katsura pond, for example, in contrast to the larger and serene Heian-style expanse in

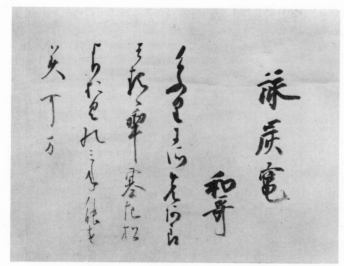

A poem and calligraphy by Gomizunoo, who may have enjoyed such a vista from the pleasant heights of Shugakuin:

> Arrayed on the peaks,
> Beyond the mist.
> More profuse than
> The cold winter pines:
> Smoking charcoal kilns.

Trail of irregular stepping stones skirting the pond near the Shōkintei, Katsura.

front of the Old Shoin, uses a multitude of rocks in consciously symbolic arrangements. One could say that the design is deliberately intellectual and provocative. Critics have called it too loquacious and too flagrantly artful. But there is yet a kind of beauty here that surpasses anything seen at Shugakuin.

One quality skillfully employed at Katsura is the element of surprise. At several points around the house and garden we encounter aspects we do not expect. For instance, if we approach the main residence along the straight and somewhat formal approach of the Imperial Visit Walkway, we are blocked at the end by a wall of shrubbery. We must turn left, and as we do, we see a single shaped pine dramatically silhouetted against the surface of the pond at the end of a hedge allée. The entry gate is on the right, but it seems small, and hardly reveals what lies beyond. As we pass through the gateway, we become aware of the famous Palanquin Entry with the *shin*-style stone walkway and a few randomly scattered stepping stones. Our breath is taken away by the unexpected beauty of the juxtaposition. The Palanquin Entry at Shugakuin hardly compares to this brilliant visual effect. There, the palanquin with its occupant inside was brought from the garden directly into the building itself. At Katsura, when the paper paneled doors are slid aside, we find a post set right in the middle of the entryway; a palanquin could not possibly get through. How the retired emperor Gomizunoo entered the Old Shoin is not clear, but surely this treatment of a standard entry was most unexpected.

Passing through the Palanquin Entry area, we encounter the Second Room of the Old Shoin, a starkly simple room without the usual thick lintels encircling the walls. The partition panels are white paper decorated with a pale yellow crest of paulownia leaves. In the adjoining First Room, the *tokonoma* alcove is very plain and the transoms between the rooms are mere vertical slats. In both spaces, there is no extraordinary ornamentation. However, when the sliding panels

of the east wall are opened, the rooms are immediately enlivened by the garden view. The natural scenery dazzles us all the more because of the dramatic contrast of interior and exterior spaces, separated only by a single sheet of paper paneling. Extending out from the Second Room is a bamboo platform exactly positioned for moon-viewing; here the building merges with the garden.

We can recall many more examples from our walk around the pond, especially the way in which scenes were quickly shifted or obscured until we arrived at just the right spot on the path to view them from. Katsura is often cited as being one of the first in the subsequently popular genre of "stroll gardens" (*kaiyūshiki teien*) in which guests were led along carefully configured paths and presented with series of views of garden elements and landscapes. The Katsura paths and stepping stones, however, are definitely not for walking and looking—the visitor would be ill-advised indeed to take his eyes off the irregular surfaces and spacings of the walkways as he makes his way through the garden. Only at the larger, flat stones positioned here and there can he safely lift his head to observe his surroundings—with the effect that the new scene is brought to him rather dramatically, fresh and whole and in a single flash.

In recent years, Katsura's main Shoin buildings and New Palace have undergone extensive restoration, revealing many details about the process of their building and the evolution of their form. The results of this analysis have also raised many questions. One of the most interesting questions, in my opinion, concerns the New Palace. It was discovered in the course of dismantling the New Palace for structural repairs that the lumber used to build it had in fact been used once before, in another structure. On the ceiling and floor boards were written records of the locations in the older building from which they had been taken. When researchers used this information to try to reconstruct what this building must have looked like they found that while in broad outline it resembled the New Palace, it faced north and could not have stood where the New Palace does. Another problem implicit here is that since the New Palace was planned expressly for retired emperor Gomizunoo's second visit to Katsura in 1663, it would have been a sign of considerable disrespect to include used lumber in its construction. Furthermore, why do we know of no structure from Gomizunoo's very first visit to Katsura, which took place in 1658?

It is my guess that this "missing" structure of 1658 was in fact what was torn down to provide lumber for the New Palace of 1663. Because the planks and ceiling boards in the older palace were already dedicated to the imperial presence, using them again in the New Palace would not have been irreverent. Probably this older palace, judging from its northern orientation, stood where the Shōkintei teahouse now does, and it helps us to know that the Shōkintei is structurally of the same period as the New Palace and not older as previously believed. Also, looking at the map of Katsura, we can see how the long stone pathway turns left off the the Imperial Visit Walkway and heads straight for the Shōkintei, on the other side of the pond. In Katsura's earlier years, when there were two separate ponds, this section was linked to the opposite shore by land and must have served as the pathway Gomizunoo used to reach the palace of 1658 that once occupied the site.

I want to emphasize that nothing is at all certain about this conclusion. But such historical puzzles—and there are many—do cast a whole new light on Katsura. We realize that what we see at Katsura, particularly in the various walkways and approaches and their complex styles, is a composite work, and that until we do further study and restoration of the garden and pavilions we won't know exactly how all the many pieces were pulled together. It is doubtful that we will ever have as clear an idea about the whole form of Katsura as we do about that of Shugakuin. The singular efforts of the retired emperor Gomizunoo have given that spacious country retreat in the hills a distinct character reflecting the tastes and personality of its owner. Still, the almost mysterious quality of Katsura's beauty is unarguably made all the more intriguing by our inability to know exactly how it was produced.

Bibliography

Bring, Mitchell, and Wayembergh, Josse. *Japanese Gardens: Design and Meaning.* New York: McGraw-Hill, 1981.

Engel, Heinrich. *The Japanese House: A Tradition for Contemporary Architecture.* Tokyo and Rutland, Vt.: Tuttle, 1964.

Fujioka Michio. *Japanese Residences and Gardens: A Tradition of Integration.* Photographs by Kazunori Tsunenari. Translated by H. Mack Horton. Tokyo and New York: Kodansha International, 1982.

Hayakawa, Masao. *The Garden Art of Japan.* Translated by Richard L. Gage. Heibonsha Survey of Japanese Art, vol. 28. New York and Tokyo: Weatherhill and Heibonsha, 1973.

Hirai, Kiyoshi. *Feudal Architecture of Japan.* Translated and adapted by Hiroaki Sato and Jeannine Ciliotta. Heibonsha Survey of Japanese Art, vol. 13. New York and Tokyo: Weatherhill and Heibonsha, 1973.

Holborn, Mark. *The Ocean in the Sand—Japan: From Landscape to Garden.* Boulder, Colo.: Shambhala, 1978.

Ishimoto, Yasuhiro. *Katsura: Tradition and Creation in Japanese Architecture.* Texts by Walter Gropius and Kenzo Tange. Translated by Charles Terry. New Haven: Yale University Press, 1960.

Ito, Teiji. *The Elegant Japanese House: Traditional Sukiya Architecture.* New York and Tokyo: Walker and Weatherhill, 1969.

———. *Space and Illusion in the Japanese Garden.* Photographs by Sosei Kuzunishi. Translated and adapted by Ralph Friedrich and Masajiro Shimamura. New York and Tokyo: Weatherhill and Tankosha, 1973.

———. *Imperial Gardens of Japan.* Photographs by Takeji Iwamiya. 2nd edition. New York and Tokyo: Weatherhill and Tankosha, 1978.

Kuck, Loraine. *The World of the Japanese Garden.* Photographs by Takeji Iwamiya. New York and Tokyo: Walker and Weatherhill, 1968.

Naitō, Akira. *Katsura: A Princely Retreat.* Photographs by Takeshi Nishikawa. Translated by Charles S. Terry. Tokyo and New York: Kodansha International, 1977.

Okawa, Naomi. *Edo Architecture: Katsura and Nikko.* Photographs by Chuji Hirayama. Translated and adapted by Alan Woodhull and Akito Miyamoto. Heibonsha Survey of Japanese Art, vol. 20. New York and Tokyo: Weatherhill and Heibonsha, 1975.

Paine, Robert T., and Soper, Alexander C. *The Art and Architecture of Japan.* 3rd edition. New York: Penguin Books, 1981.

Shigemori, Kanto. *Japanese Gardens: Islands of Serenity.* Tokyo: Japan Publications, 1971.

Treib, Marc, and Herman, Ron. *A Guide to the Gardens of Kyoto.* Tokyo: Shufunotomo, 1980.

定価3,700円
in Japan